Made from scratch

VEGETARIAN

EVERYDAY
EASY
HOME
COOKING

This edition published by Parragon Books Ltd in 2014 and distributed by

Parragon Inc.
440 Park Avenue South, 13th Floor
New York, NY 10016
www.parragon.com/lovefood

LOVE FOOD is an imprint of Parragon Books Ltd

ISBN 978-1-4723-2999-8

Printed in China

Cover photography by Ian Garlick
Design by Geoff Borin
New photography by Noel Murphy
New home economy by Sue Henderson
New recipes by Teresa Goldfinch
Introduction and notes by Sarah Bush
Edited by Fiona Biggs
Nutritional analysis by Fiona Hunter

Notes for the Reader
This book uses standard kitchen measuring spoons and cups. All spoon and cup
measurements are level unless otherwise indicated. Unless otherwise stated,
milk is assumed to be whole, eggs are large, individual vegetables are medium,
and pepper is freshly ground black pepper. Unless otherwise stated, all root
vegetables should be peeled prior to using.

Garnishes, decorations, and serving suggestions are all optional and not
necessarily included in the recipe ingredients or method. Any optional
ingredients and seasoning to taste are not included in the nutritional analysis. The
times given are only an approximate guide. Preparation times differ according
to the techniques used by different people and the cooking times may also vary
from those given. Optional ingredients, variations, or serving suggestions have
not been included in the time calculations.

Contents

Introduction

There are many misconceptions surrounding a vegetarian diet but, put simply, someone following this program removes meat, fish, and poultry from their meals and replaces them with vegetables, grains, pasta, beans, fresh fruit, and nuts. Today, more and more people are considering replacing two or three dinners a week with a vegetarian alternative—while others may have decided to convert completely.

Equally, almost all of us will know someone within our family circle or friends who is a vegetarian, so it is important to understand the basic principles when cooking for them.

Benefits of a vegetarian diet

You may be surprised, but the Western diet used to consist mainly of cereals, beans, and vegetables because most people grew their own food or bought it locally, and meat or poultry was considered a luxury only for special occasions. This high-fiber, low-fat, low-sugar, low-salt diet was far healthier for us, and illnesses that are common today were rare. The availability of mass-produced processed foods has made our lives easier, but has created more of a concern for our health.

New inspirations

Today, being vegetarian is much easier than it was in the past. For a start, there are many more ingredients available in our supermarkets, health-food stores, and ethnic food stores. Many other cultures, whose diets tend to revolve more around vegetables, are increasingly influencing our diets, and we can draw on spicy seasonings from Asia, robust flavors from the Mediterranean, and exciting grain dishes from Africa. Traveling to vacation destinations farther afield has encouraged people to sample the unfamiliar and increased a desire to cook similar dishes back home. Restaurants are more aware of the changing trends of eating and include meatless choices on their menus, which are enjoyed by vegetarians and nonvegetarians alike.

Explore your local ethnic food stores to find a range of exciting ingredients and spices.

Vegetarians and the environment

The range of fresh produce today is increasing, with growers and producers tempting us with new foods. Growing our own vegetables, fruit, and herbs is more popular and farmers' markets spring up regularly in towns all over the country. By shopping locally, we support small businesses and help lessen our environmental impact. A supply of fresh, organically grown vegetables, fruit, and salads are just on our doorstep—a boon to the vegetarian diet. Sometimes you pay a premium for this because harvesting is done on a smaller scale, often by hand, instead of using large-scale machinery; however, if you're not buying expensive meat and poultry items each week, you'll be spending less.

Vegetarians and vegans

When considering the pros and cons of changing your eating habits, you should investigate the various approaches to vegetarian food. Some people consider themselves vegetarian yet they eat fish, and others will eat chicken. Then there are those who follow a vegan diet and only eat foods of plant origin and, therefore, don't eat milk, butter, eggs, or even honey. Whichever route you choose, variety is the key to maintaining a balanced diet.

The recipes included in this book do not include any meat or fish products, but may contain dairy, such as eggs, milk, and cheese, so are not suitable for vegans, unless specified.

Pea & Herb Soup *8*

Eggplant Pâté *10*

Spicy Zucchini Soup *12*

Feta Cheese & Herb Dip *14*

Vegetable & Corn Chowder *16*

Avocado Dip *18*

Spicy Pea Soup *20*

Mini Roasted Vegetable Kabobs *22*

Roasted Squash Soup *24*

Blue Cheese & Herb Pâté *26*

White Bean Soup *28*

Batter-Fried Vegetables *30*

Thai Noodle Soup *32*

Broiled Cheese Kabobs *34*

Soups & Appetizers

Pea & Herb Soup

 SERVES 4   PREP TIME: 15 minutes plus chilling   COOKING TIME: 15–20 minutes

nutritional information per serving	277 cal, 22g fat, 8g sat fat, 4g total sugars, 0.2g salt

This elegant soup is delicious hot or chilled.

INGREDIENTS

2 tablespoons butter
6 scallions, chopped
1 celery stalk, finely chopped
2½ cups frozen peas or fresh shelled peas
3 cups vegetable stock
2 tablespoons chopped fresh dill
1 tablespoon snipped fresh chives
2 cups arugula
2 tablespoons crème fraîche or Greek-style yogurt
salt and pepper
breadsticks, to serve

basil oil
½ bunch of basil
1 cup olive oil

1. Melt the butter in a saucepan over medium heat. Add the scallions and celery, cover, and cook for 5 minutes, until soft. Add the peas and stock, bring to a boil, and simmer for 10 minutes. Remove from the heat. Cover and let cool for 20 minutes.

2. To make the basil oil, remove the stems from the basil and discard. Place the leaves in a food processor with half the oil and blend to a puree. Add the remaining oil and blend again. Transfer to a small bowl.

3. Add the dill, chives, and arugula to the soup. Blend with a handheld immersion blender until smooth. Stir in the crème fraîche. If serving warm, heat through gently without boiling, then season to taste.

4. Ladle into four warm bowls and drizzle with the basil oil. Serve immediately, with breadsticks on the side. If serving chilled, let cool completely, then chill in the refrigerator for at least 1 hour before checking the seasoning and serving.

1

2

3

COOK'S NOTE
Any leftover basil oil can be stored in the refrigerator for 3-4 days and used for drizzling over salads or ciabatta or tossing with pasta.

Eggplant Pâté

 SERVES 6

 PREP TIME:
10 minutes
plus cooling

 COOKING TIME:
1¼ hours

nutritional information
per serving 73 cal, 7.5g fat, 1g sat fat, 1g total sugars, trace salt

Also known as Poor Man's Caviar because the humble eggplant, when prepared this way, tastes so delicious!

INGREDIENTS

2 large eggplants
¼ cup extra virgin olive oil
2 garlic cloves,
finely chopped
¼ cup lemon juice
salt and pepper
2 tablespoons coarsely chopped
fresh flat-leaf parsley, to garnish
6 crispbreads, to serve

1. Preheat the oven to 350°F. Score the skins of the eggplants with the point of a sharp knife, without piercing the flesh, and place them on a baking sheet. Bake for 1¼ hours, or until soft.

2. Remove the eggplants from the oven and let stand until cool enough to handle. Cut them in half and, using a spoon, scoop out the flesh into a bowl. Mash the flesh thoroughly.

3. Gradually beat in the olive oil, then stir in the garlic and lemon juice. Season with salt and pepper. Cover with plastic wrap and store in the refrigerator until required. Sprinkle with the parsley and serve with crispbreads.

1
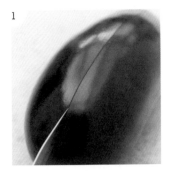

2

3

Spicy Zucchini Soup

 SERVES 4   PREP TIME: 10 minutes   COOKING TIME: 20 minutes

nutritional information per serving	195 cal, 6g fat, 0.7g sat fat, 0.8g total sugars, 1g salt

A squeeze of lime added to this light, fresh-tasting soup makes all the difference.

INGREDIENTS

2 tablespoons vegetable oil

4 garlic cloves, thinly sliced

1–2 tablespoons mild chili powder

¼ –½ teaspoon ground cumin

6½ cups vegetable stock

2 zucchini, cut into bite-size chunks

¼ cup long-grain rice

salt and pepper

fresh oregano sprigs, to garnish

lime wedges, to serve

1. Heat the oil in a heavy saucepan. Add the garlic and cook for 2 minutes, or until softened. Add the chili powder and cumin and cook over medium–low heat for 1 minute.

2. Stir in the stock, zucchini, and rice, then cook over medium–high heat for 10 minutes, or until the zucchini is just tender and the rice is cooked through. Season with salt and pepper.

3. Ladle into warm bowls, garnish with oregano sprigs, and serve immediately with lime wedges.

1
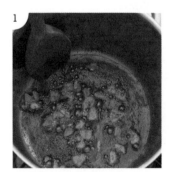

2

2

Feta Cheese & Herb Dip

 SERVES 5

 PREP TIME:
5 minutes
plus chilling

 COOKING TIME:
No cooking

nutritional information per serving	117 cal, 10g fat, 5g sat fat, 0.3g total sugars, 1g salt

This quickly made dip is also great served as an accompaniment to vegetable kabobs and baked potatoes.

INGREDIENTS

⅔ cup vegetarian low-fat cream cheese

3 tablespoons water

1 tablespoon olive oil

⅔ cup crumbled, drained vegetarian feta cheese

1 large lemon

3 tablespoons coarsely chopped fresh mint

3 tablespoons coarsely chopped fresh dill

pepper

a selection of vegetable sticks, to serve

1. Put the cream cheese, water, and oil in a food processor and process until smooth. Add the feta cheese and process briefly to combine, but make sure there are still some small lumps remaining. Transfer to a bowl.

2. Pare the zest from the lemon, using a zester. Stir the zest into the dip with the mint and dill. Season with pepper. Cover and chill for at least 30 minutes to let the flavors develop. Serve with a selection of vegetable sticks for dipping.

1

1

2

GET AHEAD

The dip and vegetable sticks can be prepared a day ahead and kept in the refrigerator.

Vegetable & Corn Chowder

 SERVES 4   PREP TIME: 10 minutes    COOKING TIME: 25–30 minutes

nutritional information per serving	363 cal, 16g fat, 8g sat fat, 14g total sugars, 0.8g salt

Chowder is traditionally from New England and is another name for a thick, hearty soup.

INGREDIENTS

1 tablespoon vegetable oil

1 red onion, diced

1 red bell pepper, seeded and diced

3 garlic cloves, crushed

2 cups peeled, diced Yukon gold or white round potatoes

2 tablespoons all-purpose flour

2½ cups whole milk

1¼ cups vegetable stock

¾ cup broccoli florets

1 (11-ounce) can corn kernels, drained

⅔ cup shredded vegetarian cheddar cheese

salt and pepper

1. Heat the oil in a large saucepan. Add the onion, red bell pepper, garlic, and potatoes and sauté over low heat, stirring frequently, for 2–3 minutes.

2. Stir in the flour and cook, stirring, for 30 seconds. Gradually stir in the milk and stock.

3. Add the broccoli and corn kernels. Bring the mixture to a boil, stirring continuously, then reduce the heat and simmer for about 20 minutes, or until all the vegetables are tender.

4. Stir in ½ cup of the cheese until it melts. Season to taste and ladle into warm bowls. Garnish with the remaining cheese and serve immediately.

1

2

3

GOES WELL WITH
Serve with crusty sourdough or whole-grain bread for a satisfying lunch.

Avocado Dip

 SERVES 4

 PREP TIME:
10 minutes

 COOKING TIME:
No cooking

nutritional information per serving	192 cal, 19g fat, 4g sat fat, 1g total sugars, trace salt

When choosing avocados for this great-tasting dip, go for the crinkly-skinned ones, which have a better flavor. Check the ripeness, they should just give slightly when pressed gently with your thumb.

INGREDIENTS

2 large avocados
juice of 1–2 limes
2 large garlic cloves, crushed
1 teaspoon mild chili powder, or to taste, plus extra to garnish
salt and pepper

1. Cut the avocados in half. Remove the pits and skin and discard.

2. Place the avocado flesh in a food processor with the juice of 1 or 2 limes, according to taste. Add the garlic and chili powder and process until smooth.

3. Season with salt and pepper. Transfer to a serving bowl, garnish with chili powder, and serve.

1

2

3

SOMETHING
DIFFERENT
Add some diced,
seeded tomatoes
or cucumber to
the mixture for
added crunch.

Spicy Pea Soup

 SERVES 4   PREP TIME: 5 minutes   COOKING TIME: 35–40 minutes

nutritional information per serving	235 cal, 6g fat, 0.8g sat fat, 2g total sugars, trace salt

Just the recipe when you want a simple soup packed with great flavors.

INGREDIENTS

4 cups water

1¼ cups pigeon peas or black-eyed peas

1 teaspoon paprika

½ teaspoon chili powder

½ teaspoon ground turmeric

2 tablespoons ghee or vegetable oil

1 fresh green chile, seeded and finely chopped

1 teaspoon cumin seeds

3 curry leaves, roughly torn

1 teaspoon sugar

salt

1 teaspoon garam masala, to garnish

1. Bring the water to a boil in a large, heavy saucepan. Add the dried peas, cover, and simmer, stirring occasionally, for 25 minutes.

2. Stir in the paprika, chili powder, and turmeric, replace the lid, and cook for an additional 10 minutes, or until the peas are tender.

3. Meanwhile, heat the ghee in a small skillet. Add the chile, cumin seeds, and curry leaves and cook, stirring continuously, for 1 minute.

4. Add the spice mixture to the peas. Stir in the sugar and season with salt. Ladle into warm bowls, garnish with garam masala, and serve immediately.

FREEZING TIP
If you find a fresh supply of curry leaves, it's worth freezing them in a zip-topped bag to save for another dish that calls for the ingredient.

Mini Roasted Vegetable Kabobs

 SERVES 4

 PREP TIME:
10 minutes

 COOKING TIME:
25–30 minutes

nutritional information per serving	135 cal, 8g fat, 2g sat fat, 10g total sugars, 0.2g salt

Roasting vegetables in the oven brings out their natural sweetness and the pieces stay in neat shapes, too.

INGREDIENTS

1 red bell pepper, seeded
1 yellow bell pepper, seeded
1 large zucchini
1 eggplant
2 tablespoons olive oil
3 garlic cloves, crushed
salt and pepper

dip
2 tablespoons chopped fresh dill
2 tablespoons chopped fresh mint
1 cup plain yogurt

1. Preheat the oven to 400°F. Cut the vegetables into ¾-inch chunks. Place in a roasting pan large enough to hold them in a single layer.

2. Mix together the olive oil and garlic and drizzle the mixture over the vegetables. Season well with salt and pepper, then toss together. Roast for 25–30 minutes, until tender and lightly charred.

3. Meanwhile, stir the dill and mint into the yogurt. Spoon into four serving bowls.

4. When the vegetables are cool enough to handle, divide them among 12 long toothpicks or short skewers. Serve warm or cold with the bowls of dip on the side.

1

2

3

BE PREPARED
Cut the vegetables into
chunks in advance and
marinate for several
hours or overnight.

Roasted Squash Soup

 SERVES 4 PREP TIME: 20 minutes COOKING TIME: 1 hour

nutritional information per serving	548 cal, 26g fat, 13g sat fat, 16g total sugars, 1.4g salt

A comforting, velvety textured soup that's perfect for freezing.

INGREDIENTS

1 butternut squash, cut into small chunks

2 onions, cut into wedges

2 tablespoons olive oil

2 garlic cloves, crushed

3–4 fresh thyme sprigs, leaves removed

4 cups vegetable stock

⅔ cup crème fraîche or Greek-style yogurt

salt and pepper

snipped fresh chives, to garnish

toasts

1 French bread, thinly sliced diagonally

½ cup grated vegetarian hard cheese

1. Preheat the oven to 375°F. Put the squash, onions, oil, garlic, and thyme leaves in a roasting pan. Toss together and spread out in a single layer. Roast for 50–60 minutes, stirring occasionally, until the vegetables are tender and caramelized in places.

2. Transfer the vegetables to a saucepan. Add half the stock and puree with a handheld immersion blender until smooth. Alternatively, blend in a food processor, then transfer to a saucepan. Stir in the remaining stock and crème fraîche. Season with salt and pepper, and heat through gently.

3. To make the toasts, preheat the broiler to high. Toast the sliced French bread under the preheated broiler for 1–2 minutes on each side, until pale golden. Sprinkle with the cheese and return to the broiler for an additional 30–40 seconds, until melted and bubbling.

4. Ladle the soup into four warm bowls and sprinkle with chives to garnish. Serve immediately with the cheese toasts on the side.

Blue Cheese & Herb Pâté

 SERVES 4   PREP TIME: 15 minutes plus chilling   COOKING TIME: 1 minute

nutritional information per serving	509 cal, 42g fat, 25g sat fat, 5g total sugars, 1.3g salt

If you need something to serve as an appetizer or pack for a picnic, this pâté is ideal.

INGREDIENTS

⅔ cup vegetarian low-fat cream cheese

1½ cups Greek-style yogurt

1 cup crumbled vegetarian blue cheese

⅓ cup dried cranberries, finely chopped

⅓ cup chopped fresh herbs, such as parsley, chives, dill, and tarragon

6 tablespoons butter

2 tablespoons chopped walnuts

whole-grain toast or breadsticks, to serve

1. Beat the cream cheese to soften, then gradually beat in the yogurt until smooth. Add the blue cheese, cranberries, and herbs. Stir together. Spoon the mixture into four ⅔-cup ramekins (individual ceramic dishes) or small dishes and carefully smooth the tops.

2. Clarify the butter by gently heating it in a small saucepan until melted. Skim any foam off the surface and discard. Carefully pour the clear yellow top layer into a small bowl, leaving the milky liquid in the pan. The yellow layer is the clarified butter. Discard the liquid left in the pan.

3. Pour a little of the clarified butter over the top of each pâté and sprinkle with the walnuts. Chill for at least 30 minutes, until firm. Serve with whole-grain toast.

1    1    3

SOMETHING
DIFFERENT
The blue cheese
can be replaced
with tangy
vegetarian goat
cheese, if you
prefer.

White Bean Soup

 SERVES 4

 PREP TIME:
10 minutes
plus soaking

 COOKING TIME:
2 hours 20 minutes

nutritional information per serving	384 cal, 18g fat, 2.5g sat fat, 1.5g total sugars, trace salt

A traditional Italian rustic soup from Tuscany. Prepare it the day before because the flavors will improve.

INGREDIENTS

1 cup dried cannellini beans, soaked in cold water to cover overnight

6½ cups vegetable stock

4 ounces dried corallini, conchigliette piccole, or other soup pasta

⅓ cup olive oil

2 garlic cloves, finely chopped

¼ cup chopped fresh flat-leaf parsley

salt and pepper

fresh crusty bread, to serve

1. Drain the soaked beans, rinse, and place them in a large, heavy saucepan. Add the stock and bring to a boil. Partly cover the pan, then reduce the heat and simmer for 2 hours, or until tender.

2. Transfer about half the beans and a little of the stock to a food processor or blender and process to a smooth puree. Return the puree to the pan and stir well to mix. Return to a boil.

3. Add the pasta, return to a boil, and cook for 10 minutes, or according to the package directions, until tender.

4. Meanwhile, heat ¼ cup of the olive oil in a small saucepan. Add the garlic and cook over low heat, stirring frequently, for 4–5 minutes, or until golden. Stir the garlic mixture into the soup and add the parsley. Season with salt and pepper and ladle into warm bowls. Drizzle with the remaining olive oil and serve immediately with crusty bread.

1

2

3

GOES WELL WITH
Salad greens
tossed with
balsamic dressing
and topped
with shavings
of cheese.

Batter-Fried Vegetables

 SERVES 4

 PREP TIME:
20 minutes

 COOKING TIME:
15 minutes

nutritional information per serving	236 cal, 12g fat, 1.5g sat fat, 4g total sugars, 0.6g salt

Serve these crunchy vegetable fritters piping hot as a snack or part of an Indian-inspired meal.

INGREDIENTS

⅓ cup chickpea (besan) flour
½ teaspoon salt
1 teaspoon chili powder
1 teaspoon baking powder
1½ teaspoons white cumin seeds
1 teaspoon pomegranate seeds
1¼ cups water
¼ bunch of cilantro, finely chopped, plus extra sprigs to garnish

vegetables of your choice
cauliflower, cut into small florets; onions, cut into rings; potatoes, sliced; eggplants, sliced; or fresh spinach leaves
vegetable oil, for deep-frying

1. Sift the chickpea flour into a large bowl. Add the salt, chili powder, baking powder, cumin, and pomegranate seeds and blend together well. Pour in the water and beat well to form a smooth batter. Add the chopped cilantro and mix well, then set aside.

2. Dip the prepared vegetables into the batter, carefully shaking off any excess.

3. Heat enough oil for deep-frying in a wok, deep-fat fryer, or a large, heavy saucepan until it reaches 350°F, or until a cube of bread browns in 30 seconds. Using tongs, place the battered vegetables in the oil and deep-fry, in batches, turning once.

4. Repeat this process until all of the batter has been used. Transfer the battered vegetables to crumpled paper towels and drain thoroughly. Garnish with cilantro sprigs and serve immediately.

1

1

1

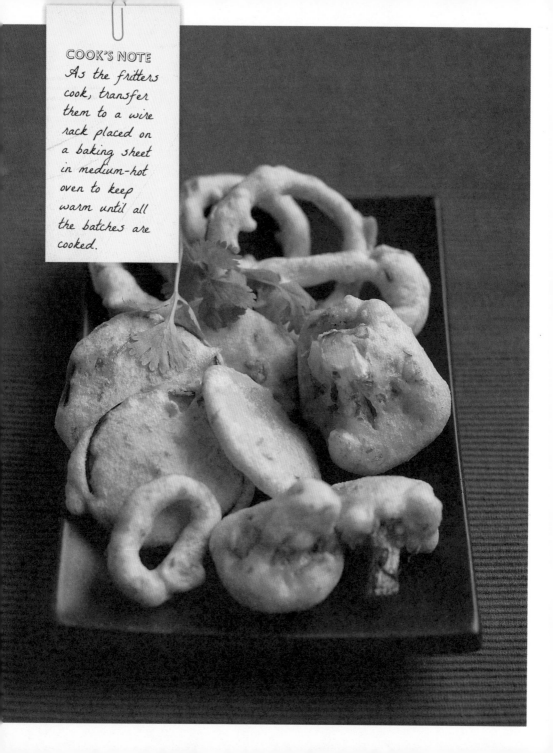

COOK'S NOTE

As the fritters cook, transfer them to a wire rack placed on a baking sheet in medium-hot oven to keep warm until all the batches are cooked.

Thai Noodle Soup

 SERVES 4   PREP TIME:
10 minutes
plus soaking   COOKING TIME:
15 minutes

nutritional information per serving	177 cal, 5.5g fat, 0.4g sat fat, 2g total sugars, 0.9g salt

Try this light, spicy soup at the beginning of a Thai-inspired meal—it will awaken the taste buds. Shiitake mushrooms provide an authentic flavor and are available in larger supermarkets or Asian stores.

INGREDIENTS

½ ounce dried shiitake mushrooms
5 cups vegetable stock
1 tablespoon peanut oil
4 scallions, sliced
8 baby corn, sliced
2 garlic cloves, crushed
2 fresh kaffir lime leaves, chopped
2 tablespoons red curry paste
3 ounces rice vermicelli noodles
1 tablespoon light soy sauce
2 tablespoons chopped cilantro, to garnish

1. Place the mushrooms in a bowl, cover with the vegetable stock, and let soak for 20 minutes.

2. Heat the peanut oil in a saucepan over medium heat. Add the scallions, baby corn, garlic, and kaffir lime leaves. Sauté for 3 minutes to soften.

3. Add the red curry paste and the soaked mushrooms and their soaking liquid. Bring to a boil and simmer for 5 minutes, stirring occasionally.

4. Add the noodles and soy sauce to the red curry mixture in the pan. Return the pan to a boil and simmer for an additional 4 minutes, until the noodles are just cooked. Ladle into warm bowls, garnish with the chopped cilantro, and serve immediately.

1

2

3

SOMETHING DIFFERENT
Use one or two ears
of corn instead of
baby corn. Stand
the cobs upright on
a board and, with a
sharp knife, cut down
from the top to remove
all the kernels.

Broiled Cheese Kabobs

 SERVES 4

 PREP TIME: 10 minutes

 COOKING TIME: 8–10 minutes

nutritional information per serving	338 cal, 24g fat, 10g sat fat, 2.5g total sugars, 1.2g salt

Mozzarella is the perfect choice for mini kabobs because it keeps its shape when broiled.

INGREDIENTS

7 ounces vegetarian mozzarella or Muenster cheese

1 garlic clove, crushed

1 fennel bulb, thinly sliced

1 small red onion, thinly sliced

1 (15-ounce) can cannellini beans, drained

1–2 tablespoons balsamic vinegar, to serve

dressing

finely grated rind and juice of 1 lemon

3 tablespoons chopped fresh flat-leaf parsley

¼ cup olive oil

salt and pepper

1. Soak four wooden skewers in water for 30 minutes to prevent them from charring. Preheat the broiler to high. For the dressing, mix together the lemon rind and juice, parsley, and oil and season with salt and pepper.

2. Cut the cheese into ¾-inch cubes, thread onto the four presoaked wooden skewers, and brush with half the dressing.

3. Cook the skewers under the preheated broiler for 6–8 minutes, turning once, until golden.

4. Heat the remaining dressing and the garlic in a small saucepan until boiling. Combine with the fennel, onion, and beans.

5. Serve the skewers with the salad, sprinkled with a little balsamic vinegar.

2

3

4

SOMETHING DIFFERENT
If fennel is not in
season, replace it with
thinly sliced celery
stalks and use the
leafy tops as garnish.

Avocado Salad *38*

Baked Eggs with Spinach *40*

Crunchy Thai Salad *42*

Couscous with Tomatoes & Pine Nuts *44*

Zucchini Fritters with Eggs *46*

Apple & Blue Cheese Salad *48*

Mozzarella Bagels *50*

Eggplant, Bell Pepper & Basil Rolls *52*

Beets & Egg on Sourdough Bread *54*

Creamy Mushroom Crepes *56*

Tofu Cakes with Chili Dip *58*

Greek Salad Bread Bowl *60*

Spicy Polenta with Poached Eggs *62*

Couscous Salad with Roasted Butternut Squash *64*

Salads & Light Meals

Avocado Salad

 SERVES 4   PREP TIME: 10 minutes   COOKING TIME: No cooking

nutritional information per serving	290 cal, 28g fat, 5g sat fat, 4.5g total sugars, 0.1g salt

A perfect choice for a light lunch, this salad is as delightful to look at as it is to eat.

INGREDIENTS

2¼ cups mixed red and green lettuce leaves

3 cups wild arugula

4 scallions, finely diced

5 tomatoes, sliced

¼ cup walnut pieces, toasted and chopped

2 avocados

1 tablespoon lemon juice

lime dressing
1 tablespoon lime juice

1 teaspoon French mustard

1 tablespoon sour cream

1 tablespoon chopped fresh parsley or cilantro

3 tablespoons extra virgin olive oil

pinch of sugar

salt and pepper

1. Wash and drain the lettuce and arugula, if necessary. Shred all the leaves and arrange in the bottom of a large salad bowl. Add the scallions, tomatoes, and walnuts.

2. Pit, peel, and thinly slice or dice the avocados. Brush with the lemon juice to prevent discoloration, then transfer to the salad bowl. Gently mix together.

3. To make the dressing, put all the dressing ingredients in a screw-top jar and shake well. Drizzle over the top of the salad and serve immediately.

Baked Eggs with Spinach

 SERVES 4   PREP TIME: 20 minutes   COOKING TIME: 35–40 minutes

nutritional information per serving	477 cal, 39g fat, 16g sat fat, 7g total sugars, 1.1g salt

This classic dish is always a favorite for a special breakfast or a lazy weekend brunch.

INGREDIENTS

1 pound fresh spinach leaves, thoroughly washed

4 tablespoons unsalted butter, plus extra for greasing

¾ cup sliced white button mushrooms

⅓ cup pine nuts, toasted

6 scallions, chopped

4 eggs

3 tablespoons whole-wheat flour

1¼ cups milk, warmed

1 teaspoon prepared English mustard

¾ cup shredded sharp vegetarian cheddar cheese

salt and pepper

1. Preheat the oven to 375°F. Shake off any excess water from the spinach, put into a large saucepan over medium heat with only the water clinging to the leaves, and sprinkle with a little salt. Cover and cook for 2–3 minutes, or until wilted. Drain, pressing out any excess liquid, then chop and place in a greased ovenproof dish.

2. Heat 1 tablespoon of the butter in a small saucepan over medium heat, add the mushrooms, and cook for 2 minutes, stirring frequently. Add the pine nuts and scallions and cook for an additional 2 minutes. Remove from the heat, season with salt and pepper, and spread the mixture over the spinach. Reserve and keep warm.

3. Meanwhile, fill a skillet with water and bring to a boil, then reduce the heat to a gentle simmer. Carefully break an egg into a cup and slip it into the water. Add the remaining eggs and cook for 4–5 minutes, or until set. Carefully remove with a slotted spoon and arrange on top of the spinach mixture.

4. Melt the remaining butter in a saucepan and stir in the flour. Cook for 2 minutes, then remove from the heat and gradually stir in the milk. Return to the heat and cook, stirring continuously, until the mixture comes to a boil and has thickened. Stir in the mustard, then ½ cup of the cheese. Continue stirring until the cheese has melted. Season with salt and pepper, then pour the sauce over the eggs, completely covering them. Sprinkle with the remaining cheese.

5. Cook in the preheated oven for 20–25 minutes, or until piping hot and the top is golden brown and bubbling. Serve immediately.

Crunchy Thai Salad

 SERVES 4   PREP TIME: 10 minutes   COOKING TIME: No cooking

nutritional information per serving	74 cal, 3g fat, 0.5g sat fat, 8g total sugars, 1.4g salt

Crispy, crunchy, and full of flavor, this salad uses a fragrant, firm mango.

INGREDIENTS

1 slightly underipe mango

5 romaine lettuce leaves, torn into pieces

1 cup bean sprouts

handful of cilantro leaves

3 tablespoons roasted unsalted peanuts, crushed

dressing
juice of 1 lime

2 tablespoons light soy sauce

1 teaspoon light brown sugar

1 shallot, very thinly sliced

1 garlic clove, finely chopped

1 red Thai chile, thinly sliced

1 tablespoon chopped fresh mint

1. To make the dressing, mix together the lime juice, soy sauce, and sugar in a bowl, then stir in the shallot, garlic, chile, and mint.

2. Peel the mango using a sharp knife or vegetable peeler. Slice the flesh from each side and around the pit. Thinly slice or shred the flesh.

3. Place the torn lettuce, bean sprouts, cilantro leaves, and mango in a serving bowl. Gently toss together. Spoon the dressing over the top of the salad, scatter with the peanuts, and serve immediately.

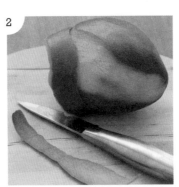

Couscous with Tomatoes & Pine Nuts

 SERVES 4

 PREP TIME:
10 minutes
plus standing

 COOKING TIME:
8 minutes

nutritional information per serving	210 cal, 14g fat, 1.5g sat fat, 2.5g total sugars, trace salt

This looks really pretty made with mixed red and yellow cherry tomatoes.

INGREDIENTS

2 cups cherry tomatoes
3 tablespoons olive oil
⅔ cup couscous
1 cup boiling water
¼ cup pine nuts, toasted
⅓ cup coarsely chopped fresh mint
finely grated zest of 1 lemon
½ tablespoon lemon juice
salt and pepper

1. Preheat the oven to 425°F. Put the tomatoes and 1 tablespoon of the oil in an ovenproof dish. Toss together, then roast for 7–8 minutes in the preheated oven, until the tomatoes are soft and the skins have burst. Let stand for 5 minutes.

2. Put the couscous in a heatproof bowl. Pour over the boiling water, cover, and let stand for 8–10 minutes, until soft and the liquid is absorbed. Fluff up with a fork.

3. Add the tomatoes and their juices, the pine nuts, mint, lemon zest, lemon juice, and the remaining oil to the couscous. Season with salt and pepper, then gently toss together. Serve warm or cold.

1

1

2

GOES WELL WITH
This goes well
with a crisp
green salad and
some vegetarian
feta cheese or
charbroiled
halloumi.

Zucchini Fritters with Eggs

 SERVES 4

 PREP TIME:
20 minutes
plus cooling

 COOKING TIME:
45 minutes

nutritional information per serving	572 cal, 33g fat, 6g sat fat, 14g total sugars, 0.8g salt

Make the caramelized onions in advance and store in the refrigerator for up to a week. If the batter for the fritters seems too thick, stir in a little extra milk.

INGREDIENTS

2 tablespoons extra virgin olive oil

5 red onions, sliced

1 tablespoon brown sugar

1⅔ cups all-purpose white flour

2½ teaspoons baking powder

1 egg, lightly beaten, plus 4 eggs for poaching or frying

1 cup milk

2 zucchini, shredded

1 cup sunflower oil

salt and pepper

1. Heat the olive oil in a large, heavy saucepan over medium heat, add the onions, and cook for 5 minutes, or until softened. Stir in the sugar and reduce the heat, cover, and cook for 30 minutes, or until the onions are deep brown in color, stirring occasionally. Season with salt and pepper and let cool.

2. To make the fritters, sift the flour and baking powder into a large bowl and make a well in the center. Mix together the beaten egg and milk and incorporate into the flour, using a wooden spoon to make a batter. Season with salt and pepper and stir in the shredded zucchini.

3. Heat the sunflower oil in a wide, deep saucepan and drop in tablespoons of the batter. Cook until golden brown on both sides, turning once. Drain on paper towels and keep warm.

4. Poach or fry the eggs, as you prefer. To serve, place three fritters on each individual plate, place an egg on top, and spoon some of the caramelized onions over the eggs. Serve immediately.

Apple & Blue Cheese Salad

 SERVES 2 PREP TIME: 10 minutes, plus cooling COOKING TIME: 5 minutes

nutritional information per serving	410 kcals, 33g fat, 11g sat fat, 19g total sugars, 0.7g salt

Apples caramelize better if there are fewer in the pan, so if you want to make more, cook in batches.

INGREDIENTS

1 tablespoon butter

2 tablespoons sunflower oil or canola oil

1 large red apple, such as Pink Lady, cored and cut into thin wedges

2 teaspoons honey

1½ teaspoons fresh thyme leaves

1½ tablespoons white wine vinegar

2 teaspoons whole-grain mustard

2 cups mixed salad greens

⅓ cup crumbled vegetarian blue cheese,

¼ cup walnut pieces, toasted and coarsely chopped

2 tablespoons snipped chives

salt and pepper

1. Heat the butter with 1 teaspoon of the oil in a skillet. Add the apples and cook for 2 minutes, stirring occasionally, until soft. Add the honey and thyme and continue to cook until the apples begin to caramelize. Remove from the heat.

2. Stir in the remaining oil, the vinegar, and mustard. Season with pepper and a little salt and let cool slightly.

3. Put the salad greens, cheese, walnuts, and chives in a serving bowl. Spoon the apples over the vegetables, along with the warm dressing from the skillet. Toss together and serve immediately.

1

2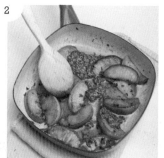

3

SOMETHING
DIFFERENT
You could use
firm, ripe pears
instead of
apples, and
toasted pine
nuts instead
of walnuts.

Mozzarella Bagels

 SERVES 4

 PREP TIME:
10 minutes

 COOKING TIME:
20 minutes

nutritional information
per serving   419 cal, 19g fat, 7g sat fat, 7g total sugars, 1.5g salt

*A really filling start to the day, the quantities
can easily be increased to feed a larger crowd.
Swap the basil leaves for arugula, if you prefer.*

INGREDIENTS

½ eggplant, thinly sliced
3–4 tablespoons olive oil
4 onion bagels or plain bagels
6 ounces vegetarian mozzarella
cheese, sliced
1 beefsteak tomato, thinly sliced
salt and pepper
6–8 fresh basil leaves, torn in half
if large, to serve

1. Preheat the oven to 375°F. Preheat a ridged grill pan until smoking. Brush the eggplant slices with a little of the oil, place on the pan, and cook for 2 minutes on each side, until tender and lightly charred.

2. Slice the bagels in half and drizzle the cut sides with the remaining oil. Divide the cheese slices among the bagel bottoms and arrange the slices of tomato and eggplant on top. Season with salt and pepper and replace the bagel tops.

3. Place on a baking sheet and bake in the preheated oven for 15 minutes, until the cheese has melted and the bagels are beginning to toast around the edges. Add a few fresh basil leaves to each bagel and serve immediately.

1

2

3

BE PREPARED
Get ahead by
assembling the
bagels and
placing them in
the refrigerator
the night before,
ready to put in
the oven at the
last minute.

Eggplant, Bell Pepper & Basil Rolls

 SERVES 4

 PREP TIME:
15 minutes
plus standing

 COOKING TIME:
15 minutes

nutritional information
per serving | 560 cal, 41g fat, 22g sat fat, 9g total sugars, 0.6g salt

Serve these vegetable and cheese rolls wrapped in paper napkins for fast food at home.

INGREDIENTS

1¼ cups all-purpose white flour

pinch of salt

1 cup whole milk

½ cup water

1 extra-large egg

2 tablespoons olive oil

sunflower oil, for greasing

filling

2 large eggplants

olive oil, for brushing

2 large red bell peppers, halved and seeded

1 cup vegetarian cream cheese

handful of fresh basil leaves

salt and pepper

1. For the filling, slice the eggplants lengthwise into ¼-inch thick slices, sprinkle with salt, and let drain for about 20 minutes. Rinse and dry.

2. Preheat the broiler to high. Arrange the eggplant slices on a baking sheet in a single layer, brush with olive oil, and broil until golden, turning once. Arrange the red bell peppers, cut-side down, on a baking sheet in a single layer and broil until blackened. Remove the skins and slice.

3. Sift the flour and salt into a bowl. Add the milk, water, egg, and oil and beat to a smooth, bubbly batter. Let stand for 15 minutes.

4. Lightly grease an 8-inch skillet and heat over medium heat. Pour in enough batter to just cover the skillet, swirling to cover in a thin, even layer. Cook until the underside is golden, then flip or turn with a spatula and cook the other side until golden brown.

5. Repeat this process using the remaining batter. Interleave the cooked crepes with paper towels and keep warm.

6. Arrange the pancakes in pairs, slightly overlapping. Spread with cheese, top with the eggplants, red bell peppers, and basil, and season with salt and pepper. Roll up firmly from one short side. Cut in half diagonally and serve immediately.

Beets & Egg on Sourdough Bread

 SERVES 4   *PREP TIME:*
10 minutes   *COOKING TIME:*
12–15 minutes

nutritional information per serving	404 cal, 24g fat, 4g sat fat, 14g total sugars, 1.4g salt

Try this traditional combination of ruby-red beets and chopped egg served on sourdough bread for a great lunch dish.

INGREDIENTS

4 eggs

8 cooked beets (fresh or vacuum-packed without vinegar)

2 teaspoons sugar

5 teaspoons cider vinegar

4 slices sourdough bread (from a long oval loaf)

⅓ cup olive oil

1 tablespoon Dijon mustard

3 tablespoons chopped fresh dill, plus extra sprigs to garnish

salt and pepper

1. Preheat the broiler to a medium–high setting. Boil the eggs in a saucepan of boiling water for 5 minutes, then drain, shell, and chop them. Set aside. Dice the beets finely and place in a small bowl. Mix in half the sugar, 1 teaspoon of the cider vinegar, and season with salt and pepper.

2. Brush the bread with a little olive oil and toast on one side on the rack in the broiler pan for 2–3 minutes, until crisp and golden.

3. Meanwhile, trickle 1 teaspoon of the remaining oil over the beets. Beat together the remaining cider vinegar, mustard, and remaining sugar and season with salt and pepper. Gradually beat in the remaining oil to make a thick dressing. Stir in the dill and taste for seasoning—it should be sweet and mustardy, with a sharpness—add more sugar or vinegar, if you desire.

4. Turn over the bread and top with the beets after first stirring them, covering the slices right up to the crusts. Glaze the beets under the broiler for 2–3 minutes, until browned in places.

5. Cut the slices in half or quarters and top with egg. Drizzle with a little dressing, garnish with the dill sprigs, and serve immediately.

Creamy Mushroom Crepes

 SERVES 2

 PREP TIME: 10 minutes

 COOKING TIME: 5 minutes

nutritional information per serving	562 cal, 39g fat, 15g sat fat, 8g total sugars, 0.6g salt

This really quick mushroom filling makes a perfect partner for whole-wheat crepes.

INGREDIENTS

¼ cup light olive oil

4 cups sliced cremini mushrooms

1 teaspoon dried thyme or 2 teaspoons fresh thyme leaves

2 tablespoons chopped fresh flat-leaf parsley

1 cup reduced-fat crème fraîche

⅔ cup whole-wheat flour

1 teaspoon baking powder

1 egg

1 cup low-fat milk

salt and pepper

1. Heat 2 tablespoons of the oil in a skillet. Add the mushrooms, thyme, and half the parsley. Season with salt and pepper and cook over high heat for 2 minutes. Stir in the crème fraîche.

2. Beat together the flour, baking powder, egg, and milk in a bowl and season with salt and pepper. Heat ½ teaspoon of the remaining oil in an 8-inch nonstick skillet until hot. Add one-quarter of the batter, tilting the skillet to cover the bottom. Cook over high heat for 30 seconds, then flip the crepe and cook for an additional minute. Slide it onto a warm plate. Repeat to make another three crepes.

3. Spoon one-quarter of the mushroom mixture into the center of each crepe and fold over. Sprinkle with the remaining parsley and serve.

1

2

3

BE PREPARED
Make and fill the crepes in advance and arrange in an ovenproof dish. Cover with aluminum foil and reheat in a medium-hot oven until the filling is bubbling.

Tofu Cakes with Chili Dip

 SERVES 4

 PREP TIME:
10 minutes
plus chilling

 COOKING TIME:
10–12 minutes

nutritional information per serving	226 cal, 10g fat, 1.5g sat fat, 5g total sugars, 0.7g salt

Similar to a fish cake, this Thai favorite would also make a great appetizer or snack with drinks.

INGREDIENTS

2 cups coarsely grated firm tofu

1 lemongrass stalk, finely chopped

2 garlic cloves, chopped

1-inch piece fresh ginger, grated

2 kaffir lime leaves, finely chopped (optional)

2 shallots, finely chopped

2 fresh red chiles, seeded and finely chopped

¼ cup chopped cilantro

¾ cup all-purpose flour, plus extra for dusting

½ teaspoon salt

vegetable oil, for cooking

chili dip

3 tablespoons white distilled vinegar

2 scallions, finely sliced

1 tablespoon sugar

2 fresh chiles, chopped

2 tablespoons chopped cilantro

pinch of salt

1. To make the chile dip, mix together all the ingredients in a small serving bowl and set aside.

2. Mix the tofu with the lemongrass, garlic, ginger, lime leaves, if using, shallots, chiles, and cilantro in a mixing bowl. Stir in the flour and salt to make a coarse, sticky paste. Cover and chill in the refrigerator for 1 hour to let the mixture become slightly firm.

3. Form the mixture into eight walnut-size balls and, using floured hands, flatten into circles. Heat enough oil to cover the bottom of a large, heavy skillet over medium heat. Cook the cakes in two batches, turning halfway through, for 4–6 minutes, or until golden brown. Drain on paper towels and serve warm with the chile dip.

Greek Salad Bread Bowl

 SERVES 2   PREP TIME: 10 minutes   COOKING TIME: 5 minutes

nutritional information per serving	655 cal, 50g fat, 18g sat fat, 11g total sugars, 4.4g salt

Crisp, toasted rustic-style bread topped with a salad that packs in the flavors.

INGREDIENTS

1 garlic clove, crushed

¼ cup olive oil

2 thick slices from a large, seeded loaf of bread

1⅓ cups diced, drained vegetarian feta cheese

pepper

¼ cucumber, finely diced

¼ cup sliced, pitted ripe black olives

4 plum tomatoes, diced

½ small onion, chopped

2 sprigs fresh mint leaves, shredded

2 sprigs fresh oregano leaves, chopped

¼ teaspoon sugar

1 heart Boston lettuce, finely shredded

½ teaspoon toasted sesame seeds

2 teaspoons pine nuts (optional)

1. Preheat the broiler to medium–high setting. Mix the garlic and olive oil in a bowl large enough to mix all the salad ingredients in.

2. Place the bread on the rack in the broiler pan. Brush lightly with the garlic oil and toast well away from the heat for 2–3 minutes, until crisp and golden. Turn over the bread and brush lightly with more oil, then toast again.

3. Add the feta cheese to the garlic oil remaining in the bowl and season with pepper (the cheese and olives usually provide enough salt). Mix in the cucumber, olives, tomatoes, onion, mint, and oregano. Sprinkle with the sugar and mix well. Finally, lightly mix in the lettuce.

4. Transfer the toasts to plates and spoon the salad and its juices over them. Sprinkle with the sesame seeds and pine nuts (if using) and serve immediately, while the toasts are hot and crisp.

Spicy Polenta with Poached Eggs

 SERVES 4

 PREP TIME: 10 minutes plus cooling

 COOKING TIME: 11–15 minutes

nutritional information per serving	414 cal, 24g fat, 11g sat fat, 1g total sugars, 1g salt

To use the polenta scraps, chop coarsely, place in a shallow ovenproof dish, brush with melted butter, and broil for 3 minutes. Serve as an unusual side dish.

INGREDIENTS

oil, for oiling

2½ cups water

1 cup instant polenta or cornmeal

1 cup freshly grated vegetarian Parmesan-style cheese

3 tablespoons butter

½–1 red chile, seeded and finely chopped

7 cups baby spinach leaves, or a mixture of baby spinach leaves and arugula leaves

2 teaspoons white wine vinegar

4 extra-large eggs

salt and pepper

1. Lightly oil a 7-inch square cake pan. Bring the water to a boil in a saucepan. Add the polenta in a thin stream and cook, stirring, over medium–low heat for 3 minutes, until thick. Stir in ⅔ cup of the cheese, 2 tablespoons of the butter, and the chile. Working quickly, transfer to the prepared pan and level the surface. Set aside for 30 minutes, until cool and firm, then cut out 4 circles with a 3½-inch pastry cutter and transfer to a baking sheet.

2. Preheat the broiler to high. Wash the spinach and place in a large saucepan with the water clinging to the leaves. Cover and cook for 2–3 minutes, until wilted, then squeeze out the excess water between two plates. Return to the pan.

3. Sprinkle the polenta circles with the remaining cheese, place under the preheated broiler, and cook for 3 minutes, until brown and bubbling on the top. Keep warm. Meanwhile, add the remaining butter to the spinach, season with salt and pepper, and heat all the way through.

4. Fill a saucepan halfway with water, add the vinegar, and bring to simmering point. Crack the eggs into cups and slide gently into the water. Poach over low heat, without letting the water boil, for 3 minutes, until the whites are firm and the yolk is still soft. Scoop out with a slotted spoon and drain briefly on paper towels.

5. To serve, place the polenta circles on four warm plates and divide the spinach among them. Top with the eggs and sprinkle with a little salt and pepper. Serve immediately.

Couscous Salad with Roasted Butternut Squash

 SERVES 4   PREP TIME: 10 minutes   COOKING TIME: 30–40 minutes

nutritional information per serving	370 cal, 13g fat, 2g sat fat, 19g total sugars, trace salt

Couscous is a Mediterranean favorite and can be cooked in many ways, including this Moroccan-inspired salad.

INGREDIENTS

2 tablespoons honey

¼ cup olive oil

1 butternut squash, peeled, seeded, and cut into ¾-inch chunks

1¼ cups couscous

1¾ cups low-sodium vegetable stock

½ cucumber, diced

1 zucchini, diced

1 red bell pepper, seeded and diced

juice of ½ lemon

2 tablespoons chopped fresh parsley

salt and pepper

1. Preheat the oven to 375°F. Mix half the honey with 1 tablespoon of the oil in a large bowl, add the squash, and toss well to coat. Transfer to a roasting pan and roast in the preheated oven for 30–40 minutes, until soft and golden.

2. Meanwhile, put the couscous in a heatproof bowl. Heat the stock in a saucepan and pour it over the couscous, cover, and let stand for 3 minutes. Add 1 tablespoon of the remaining oil and fork through, then stir in the diced cucumber, zucchini, and red bell pepper. Replace the lid and keep warm.

3. Whisk the remaining honey and oil with the lemon juice in a bowl and season with salt and pepper. Stir the mixture through the couscous.

4. To serve, top the couscous with the roasted squash and sprinkle with the parsley.

1

2

2

BE PREPARED
This dish can
also be made
in advance and
served cold—
great for a
picnic.

Lentil Bolognese *68*

Smoky Mushroom & Cilantro Burgers *70*

Leek, Herb & Mushroom Risotto *72*

Stir-Fried Rice with Green Vegetables *74*

Pasta with Two Cheeses & Walnuts *76*

Mediterranean Vegetables with Feta & Olives *78*

Tofu Stir-Fry *80*

Pasta with Tomato & Mascarpone Sauce *82*

Grilled Zucchini & Feta Pizza *84*

New Potato, Feta & Herb Frittata *86*

Bean & Vegetable Chili *88*

Quinoa with Roasted Vegetables *90*

Spinach Pie *92*

Mixed Nut Loaf *94*

Main Meals

Lentil Bolognese

 SERVES 4

 PREP TIME:
15 minutes

 COOKING TIME:
45–55 minutes

nutritional information per serving	500 cal, 8g fat, 1g sat fat, 16.5g total sugars, 0.3g salt

No vegetarian kitchen should be without a recipe for this popular pasta sauce.

INGREDIENTS

1 cup dried green lentils
2 tablespoons olive oil
1 large onion, chopped
2 garlic cloves, crushed
2 carrots, chopped
2 celery stalks, chopped
1 (28-ounce) can diced tomatoes
⅔ cup vegetable stock
1 red bell pepper, seeded and chopped
2 tablespoons tomato paste
2 teaspoons finely chopped fresh rosemary
1 teaspoon dried oregano
10 ounces dried spaghetti or linguine
handful of basil leaves, torn
salt and pepper
freshly grated vegetarian Parmesan-style cheese, to serve

1. Put the lentils in a saucepan and cover with cold water. Bring to a boil and simmer for about 30 minutes, or according to the package directions, until just tender. Drain well.

2. Meanwhile, heat the oil in a large saucepan. Add the onion, garlic, carrots, and celery. Cover and cook over low heat for 5 minutes. Stir in the tomatoes, stock, red bell pepper, tomato paste, rosemary, and oregano. Cover and simmer for 20 minutes, until the sauce is thickened and the vegetables are tender. Add the lentils and cook, stirring, for an additional 5 minutes. Season with salt and pepper.

3. While the sauce is cooking, bring a large saucepan of lightly salted water to a boil. Add the spaghetti, bring back to a boil, and cook according to the package directions, until tender but still firm to the bite. Drain well, then divide the spaghetti among four warm bowls. Spoon the sauce over the pasta and sprinkle with the basil leaves. Serve immediately with the grated cheese.

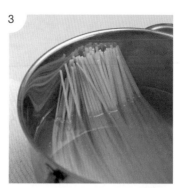

Smoky Mushroom & Cilantro Burgers

 SERVES 6

 PREP TIME: 15 minutes

 COOKING TIME: 10–15 minutes

nutritional information per serving	170 cal, 6g fat, 0.8g sat fat, 5g total sugars, 1.8g salt

Children will love helping mix and shape these vegan burgers.

INGREDIENTS

1 (15-ounce) can red kidney beans, rinsed and drained

2 tablespoons sunflower oil or vegetable oil, plus extra for brushing

1 onion, finely chopped

1⅔ cups finely chopped white button mushrooms

1 large carrot, shredded

2 teaspoons smoked paprika

¾ cup rolled oats

3 tablespoons dark soy sauce

2 tablespoons tomato paste

½ bunch of cilantro, including stems, chopped

3 tablespoons all-purpose flour

salt and pepper

to serve
soft rolls

salad greens

sliced avocado

tomato salsa or relish

1. Put the beans in a large bowl and mash as thoroughly as you can with a vegetable masher. Heat the oil in a skillet, add the onion, and sauté for 2 minutes, until translucent. Add the mushrooms, carrot, and paprika and sauté for an additional 4 minutes, until the vegetables are soft.

2. Add the sautéed vegetables to the beans with the oats, soy sauce, tomato paste, and cilantro. Season with salt and pepper and mix well. Divide into six equal portions and shape into patties, then turn in the flour to coat lightly.

3. Preheat a ridged grill pan until smoking. Lightly brush the tops of the patties with oil, then place oiled-side down on the pan. Cook over medium heat for 2–3 minutes, until lightly charred underneath. Lightly brush the tops with oil, turn, and cook for an additional 2-3 minutes on the other side. Serve hot in soft rolls with salad greens, avocado slices, and salsa.

Leek, Herb & Mushroom Risotto

 SERVES 8   PREP TIME: 15 minutes   COOKING TIME: 30–35 minutes

nutritional information per serving	243 cal, 8.5g fat, 4g sat fat, 0.5g total sugars, 0.2g salt

A filling and comforting dish. Use a mixture of cultivated and wild mushrooms instead of cremini mushrooms, if you prefer.

INGREDIENTS

4¼ cups hot vegetable stock

2 tablespoons olive oil

1 small leek, coarsely chopped

3 garlic cloves, crushed

1 tablespoon fresh thyme

4 cups sliced cremini mushrooms

1½ cups risotto rice

¾ cup dry white wine

2 tablespoons butter

½ cup freshly grated vegetarian Parmesan-style cheese

2 tablespoons snipped fresh chives, plus extra to serve

salt and pepper

arugula and vegetarian Parmesan-style cheese shavings, to garnish

1. Keep the stock hot in a saucepan set over medium heat. Heat the oil in a separate saucepan over low heat. Add the leek, garlic, and thyme and cook for 5 minutes, until soft. Add the mushrooms and continue to cook for an additional 4 minutes, until soft.

2. Stir in the rice and cook, stirring, for 1 minute, then add the wine and heat rapidly until the liquid has almost completely evaporated.

3. Add a ladleful of stock and cook over medium heat, stirring, until it is absorbed by the rice. Continue adding the stock in the same way until it is all used up and the rice is creamy, plump, and tender.

4. If the risotto is a little undercooked, add a splash of water and continue cooking until creamy. Adding extra stock may make the risotto too salty.

5. Stir in the butter, followed by the cheese and chives. Season with salt and pepper. Serve in warm bowls topped with arugula, chives, and cheese shavings.

Stir-Fried Rice with Green Vegetables

 SERVES 4 PREP TIME: 5 minutes plus cooling COOKING TIME: 20–25 minutes

nutritional information per serving	288 cal, 7g fat, 0.8g sat fat, 3g total sugars, 0.2g salt

Thai basil should not be confused with sweet basil used in many Italian dishes. Thai basil has a slight licorice flavor that complements this dish perfectly.

INGREDIENTS

1¼ cups jasmine rice

2 tablespoons vegetable oil or peanut oil

1 tablespoon green curry paste

6 scallions, sliced

2 garlic cloves, crushed

1 zucchini, cut into thin sticks

1 cup trimmed green beans

10 asparagus spears, trimmed

3–4 fresh Thai basil leaves

1. Cook the rice in lightly salted, boiling water according to the package directions. Drain well, cover, cool thoroughly, and chill.

2. Heat the oil in a wok and stir-fry the curry paste for 1 minute. Add the scallions and garlic and stir-fry for 1 minute.

3. Add the zucchini, beans, and asparagus and stir-fry for 3–4 minutes, until just tender. Break up the rice and add it to the wok. Cook, stirring continuously, for 2–3 minutes, until the rice is hot. Stir in the basil and serve immediately.

1

2

3

Pasta with Two Cheeses & Walnuts

 SERVES 4   PREP TIME: 5 minutes   COOKING TIME: 15 minutes

nutritional information per serving	838 cal, 49g fat, 20g sat fat, 5g total sugars, 0.9g salt

The perfect dish to eat curled up on the couch watching TV. Alternatively, it makes a wonderful meal for a more formal dining setting, served with a crisp salad and a glass of wine.

INGREDIENTS

12 ounces dried penne

2 cups fresh or frozen peas

⅔ cup vegetarian cream cheese with garlic and herbs

1 (6-ounce) package baby spinach leaves

1 cup diced vegetarian blue cheese

1 cup coarsely chopped walnuts

salt and pepper

1. Cook the pasta in a large saucepan of lightly salted, boiling water according to the package directions, adding the peas for the final 2 minutes. Drain, reserving ½ cup of the hot cooking liquid.

2. Return the pan to the heat. Add the reserved cooking liquid and the cream cheese. Heat, stirring, until melted and smooth.

3. Remove from the heat, then add the spinach to the pan, followed by the pasta, peas, blue cheese, and walnuts. Season with pepper and toss together, until the spinach has wilted and the cheese has started to melt. Serve immediately.

1

2

3

COOK'S NOTE
A splash of olive oil added to the cooking water helps prevent the pasta from sticking together.

Mediterranean Vegetables
with Feta & Olives

 SERVES 4   PREP TIME: 10 minutes    COOKING TIME: 20–25 minutes

nutritional information per serving	240 cal, 12g fat, 2.5g sat fat, 11g total sugars, 0.7g salt

Let the wonderful aromas wafting from the kitchen remind you of warm evenings dining alfresco.

INGREDIENTS

1 red onion, sliced into thick rings

1 small eggplant, thickly sliced

2 large mushrooms, halved

3 red bell peppers, halved and seeded

3 plum tomatoes, peeled and diced

2 garlic cloves, minced

1 tablespoon chopped fresh flat-leaf parsley

1 teaspoon chopped fresh rosemary

1 teaspoon dried thyme or dried oregano

finely grated rind of 1 lemon

¾ cup stale, coarse bread crumbs

3 tablespoons olive oil, plus extra for brushing

6–8 ripe black olives, pitted and sliced

2 tablespoons diced, drained vegetarian feta cheese (cut into ½-inch cubes)

salt and pepper

1. Preheat the broiler to medium. Put the onion, eggplant, mushrooms, and bell peppers on a large baking pan, placing the bell peppers cut-side down. Brush with a little oil. Cook under the preheated broiler for 10–12 minutes, turning the onion, eggplant, and mushrooms halfway through, until beginning to blacken. Cut into even chunks.

2. Preheat the oven to 425°F. Place the broiled vegetables in a shallow ovenproof dish and arrange the tomatoes over them. Season with salt and pepper.

3. In a bowl, combine the garlic, parsley, rosemary, thyme, and lemon rind with the bread crumbs. Season with pepper. Add the oil to bind together the mixture. Spread the bread crumb mixture over the vegetables, followed by the olives and feta cheese.

4. Bake in the preheated oven for 10–15 minutes, or until the vegetables are heated all the way through and the topping is crisp. Serve immediately.

Tofu Stir-Fry

 SERVES 2   PREP TIME: 15 minutes   COOKING TIME: 15 minutes

nutritional information per serving	738 cal, 25g fat, 4g sat fat, 33g total sugars, 4.6g salt

Try this method of dry-frying tofu, which makes the texture firm without adding extra calories and fat.

INGREDIENTS

5 ounces medium egg noodles

1 (8-ounce) package firm tofu, drained

2 tablespoons sunflower oil or vegetable oil

1 red bell pepper, seeded and thinly sliced

10 baby corn, diagonally sliced

3 cups choy sum or bok choy (1½-inch pieces)

salt

sauce

3 tablespoons tamari or dark soy sauce

3 tablespoons rice wine

3 tablespoons honey

1 tablespoon cornstarch

1 tablespoon finely grated fresh ginger

1–2 garlic cloves, crushed

1 cup water

1. Bring a large saucepan of lightly salted water to a boil. Add the noodles, bring back to a boil, and cook according to the package directions, until tender but still firm to the bite. Drain.

2. Meanwhile, cut the tofu into ½-inch slices and then into bite-size pieces. Pat dry on plenty of paper towels. Heat a nonstick or well-seasoned skillet over medium–low heat, then add the tofu and cook for 3 minutes, without moving the pieces around the skillet, until golden brown underneath. Turn and cook for an additional 2–3 minutes on the other side. Transfer to a plate.

3. To make the sauce, mix the tamari, rice wine, honey, cornstarch, ginger, and garlic together in a small bowl until well blended, then stir in the water. Set aside.

4. Heat the oil in a wok or large, heavy skillet. Add the bell pepper and baby corn and stir-fry for 3 minutes. Add the choy sum and stir-fry for an additional 2 minutes. Pour in the sauce and heat, stirring continuously, until it boils and thickens. Add the noodles and tofu and toss together over the heat for an additional 1–2 minutes, until heated through. Serve immediately.

Pasta with Tomato & Mascarpone Sauce

 SERVES 4

 PREP TIME:
15 minutes

 COOKING TIME:
30–35 minutes

nutritional information per serving	520 cal, 24g fat, 10g sat fat, 11g total sugars, 0.2g salt

With its creamy sauce and generous helping of roasted vegetables, this pasta dish will satisfy the heartiest of appetites.

INGREDIENTS

4 zucchini, coarsely chopped

2½ tablespoons olive oil

1 onion, finely chopped

1 garlic clove, crushed

1 (28-ounce) can diced tomatoes

6 sun-dried tomatoes, chopped

1 cup vegetable stock

½ teaspoon dried oregano

10 ounces dried rigatoni pasta

½ cup vegetarian mascarpone or ricotta cheese

salt and pepper

large handful of fresh basil leaves, torn into pieces

1. Preheat the oven to 400°F. Put the zucchini and 1½ tablespoons of the oil in a large ovenproof dish. Toss together and spread out in a single layer. Roast in the preheated oven for 15–20 minutes, until tender and lightly browned.

2. Meanwhile, heat the remaining oil in a saucepan. Add the onion and garlic and cook gently for 5 minutes, until soft. Add the canned tomatoes, sun-dried tomatoes, stock, and oregano. Simmer for 10 minutes, until the liquid has reduced slightly.

3. Bring a large saucepan of lightly salted water to a boil. Add the pasta, bring back to a boil, and cook according to the package directions, until tender but still firm to the bite. Drain well, then return to the pan.

4. Add the mascarpone cheese to the hot sauce and stir until melted and smooth. Season well with salt and pepper. Add to the pasta with the zucchini and the basil leaves. Toss together until the pasta is well coated in sauce. Serve immediately.

1

2

4

Grilled Zucchini & Feta Pizza

 MAKES
2 pizzas

 PREP TIME:
20 minutes
plus rising

 COOKING TIME:
15–20 minutes

nutritional information per pizza	996 cal, 42g fat, 20g sat fat, 10g total sugars, 8.6g salt

However easy it is to order a pizza, you can't beat the taste and texture of the dough when you make it yourself.

INGREDIENTS

basic pizza dough
2¼ cups white bread flour, plus extra for dusting
1 teaspoon active dry yeast
1½ teaspoons salt
¾ cup lukewarm water
1 tablespoon olive oil, plus extra for kneading

topping
1 tablespoon olive oil
1 garlic clove, crushed
1 large zucchini, sliced lengthwise
¾ cup prepared tomato-based pizza sauce
1⅓ cups crumbled, drained vegetarian feta cheese
salt and pepper
fresh mint leaves, coarsely torn, to garnish

1. Sift the flour into a mixing bowl and add the yeast and salt, making a small well in the center. Mix together the water and oil, add to the dry ingredients, and, using a rubber spatula, gradually combine all the ingredients to make a sticky dough.

2. Lightly flour the work surface and your hands and knead the dough for about 10 minutes, until it is smooth and elastic.

3. Cover the dough with some lightly oiled plastic wrap or a damp dish towel and let rise for about an hour, or until it has doubled in size.

4. Preheat the oven to 425°F. Punch down the dough to knock out the air and gently knead for about a minute, then divide into two balls. To roll out the dough, flatten each ball, then, using a rolling pin, roll out on a lightly floured surface, giving a quarter turn between each roll.

5. Place the pizza dough crusts on two baking sheets, using a rolling pin to transfer them from the work surface.

6. Heat the oil in a ridged grill pan over medium heat. Add the garlic and zucchini and cook over medium heat for 4–5 minutes, turning regularly, until softened and chargrilled. Remove with a slotted spoon and drain on paper towels.

7. Divide the pizza sauce between the two pizza crusts, spreading it almost to the edges. Place the zucchini slices on the pizza crusts, sprinkle with the cheese, and season with salt and pepper. Bake in the preheated oven for 10–12 minutes, or until the cheese is turning golden and the crusts are crisp underneath. Garnish with the fresh mint and serve immediately.

New Potato, Feta & Herb Frittata

 SERVES 4   PREP TIME: 10 minutes   COOKING TIME: 30–35 minutes

nutritional information per serving	273 cal, 19g fat, 8g sat fat, 1.5g total sugars, 1.5g salt

This chunky omelet is delicious cold as well as hot, so it's perfect for picnics and lunch boxes.

INGREDIENTS

6 new potatoes, scrubbed

3 cups baby spinach leaves

5 eggs

1 tablespoon chopped fresh dill, plus extra to garnish

1 tablespoon snipped fresh chives, plus extra to garnish

¾ cup crumbled, drained vegetarian feta cheese,

½ tablespoon butter

1 tablespoon olive oil

salt and pepper

1. Bring a saucepan of lightly salted water to a boil, add the potatoes, bring back to a boil, and cook for 25 minutes, until tender. Place the spinach in a colander and drain the potatoes over the top to wilt the spinach. Set aside until cool enough to handle.

2. Cut the potatoes lengthwise into ¼-in thick slices. Squeeze the excess water from the spinach leaves. Preheat the broiler to high.

3. Lightly beat together the eggs, dill, and chives. Season with pepper and add ½ cup of the cheese. Heat the butter and oil in an 8-inch skillet until melted and foaming. Add the potato slices and spinach and cook, stirring, for 1 minute. Pour the egg-and-cheese mixture over the vegetables.

4. Cook, stirring, over medium heat for 1 minute, until half set, then continue to cook for 2–3 minutes, without stirring, until set and golden brown underneath. Sprinkle the remaining cheese over the omlet, place under the preheated broiler, and cook for 2 minutes, until golden brown on top. Serve hot or cold, sprinkled with chives and dill.

1

3

4

SOMETHING DIFFERENT

This frittata is a great way of using up leftover boiled, baked, or roasted potatoes. Cut them into chunky pieces if they are too crumbly to slice.

Bean & Vegetable Chili

 SERVES 4   PREP TIME: 10 minutes   COOKING TIME: 20 minutes

nutritional information per serving	180 cal, 1.5g fat, 0.2g sat fat, 14g total sugars, 1.4g salt

This must be one of the most popular dishes to serve a crowd. Be careful not to go mad with the chili powder—have your favorite chili sauce available so everyone can adjust the heat level to suit.

INGREDIENTS

¼ cup vegetable stock

1 onion, coarsely chopped

1 green bell pepper, seeded and finely chopped

1 red bell pepper, seeded and finely chopped

1 teaspoon finely chopped garlic

1 teaspoon finely chopped fresh ginger

2 teaspoons ground cumin

½ teaspoon chili powder

2 tablespoons tomato paste

1 (14½-ounce) can diced tomatoes

1 (15-ounce) can kidney beans, drained and rinsed

1 (15-ounce) can black-eyed peas, drained and rinsed

salt and pepper

tortilla chips, to serve

1. Heat the stock in a large saucepan, add the onion and bell peppers, and simmer for 5 minutes, or until softened.

2. Stir in the garlic, ginger, cumin, chili powder, tomato paste, and tomatoes. Season with salt and pepper and simmer for 10 minutes.

3. Stir in the beans and peas and simmer for an additional 5 minutes, or until heated through. Serve immediately with tortilla chips.

Quinoa with Roasted Vegetables

 SERVES 2 PREP TIME: 10 minutes COOKING TIME: 40–45 minutes

nutritional information per serving	418 cal, 23g fat, 2g sat fat, 14g total sugars, 0.1g salt

Quinoa (pronounced keen-wah) is an ancient grain originating from South America.

INGREDIENTS

2 bell peppers (any color), seeded and cut into chunky pieces

1 large zucchini, cut into chunks

1 small fennel bulb, cut into slim wedges

1 tablespoon olive oil

2 teaspoons very finely chopped fresh rosemary

1 teaspoon chopped fresh thyme

⅔ cup quinoa

1½ cups vegetable stock

2 garlic cloves, crushed

3 tablespoons chopped fresh flat-leaf parsley

⅓ cup pine nuts, toasted

salt and pepper

1. Preheat the oven to 400°F. Place the bell peppers, zucchini, and fennel in a roasting pan large enough to hold the vegetables in a single layer.

2. Drizzle the olive oil over the vegetables and sprinkle with the rosemary and thyme. Season well with salt and pepper and mix well with clean hands. Roast for 25–30 minutes, until tender and lightly charred.

3. Meanwhile, place the quinoa, stock, and garlic in a saucepan. Bring to a boil, cover, and simmer for 12–15 minutes, until tender and most of the stock has been absorbed.

4. Remove the vegetables from the oven. Transfer the quinoa to the roasting pan. Add the parsley and pine nuts and toss together. Serve warm or cold.

SOMETHING
DIFFERENT
If you're unable
to buy highly
nutritious quinoa
(although it's
a very popular
grain these days)
use brown
long-grain rice
instead.

Spinach Pie

 SERVES 8

 PREP TIME:
30 minutes
plus chilling

 COOKING TIME:
60 minutes

nutritional information per serving	483 cal, 32g fat, 17g sat fat, 3g total sugars, 1.1g salt

The perfect combination of spinach and ricotta encased in crispy, flaky pastry.

INGREDIENTS

pastry dough
2¾ cups all-purpose flour, plus extra for dusting
pinch of salt
1½ sticks butter, diced, plus extra for greasing
2 egg yolks
⅓ cup ice-cold water

filling
3 cups thawed, frozen spinach (about 1 pound)
2 tablespoons olive oil
1 large onion, chopped
2 garlic cloves, finely chopped
2 eggs, lightly beaten
8 ounces vegetarian ricotta cheese
½ cup freshly grated vegetarian Parmesan-style cheese
pinch of freshly grated nutmeg
salt and pepper

1. To make the dough, sift the flour with the salt into a bowl. Add the butter and rub into the flour with your fingertips until the mixture resembles fine bread crumbs. Beat the egg yolks with the water in a small bowl. Sprinkle the liquid over the flour mixture and combine with a rubber spatula to form a dough. Shape into a ball, wrap in aluminum foil, and chill in the refrigerator for 30 minutes.

2. Meanwhile, preheat the oven to 400°F. Lightly grease a 9-inch loose-bottom tart pan. To make the filling, drain the spinach and squeeze out as much moisture as possible. Heat the oil in a large, heavy skillet over medium heat. Add the onion and cook, stirring frequently, for 5 minutes, or until softened. Add the garlic and spinach and cook, stirring occasionally, for 10 minutes. Remove from the heat and let cool slightly, then beat in the eggs (reserving a little for glazing), ricotta, and grated cheese. Season with salt and pepper and nutmeg.

3. Roll out two-thirds of the dough on a lightly floured work surface and use to line the pan. Spoon in the spinach mixture, spreading it evenly over the bottom.

4. Roll out the remaining dough on a lightly floured surface and cut into ¼-inch strips. Arrange the strips in a lattice pattern on top of the tart, pressing the ends securely to seal. Trim any excess dough. Brush with the egg to glaze and bake in the preheated oven for 45 minutes, or until golden brown. Transfer to a wire rack to cool slightly before removing from the pan.

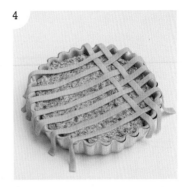

Mixed Nut Loaf

 MAKES
1 loaf

 PREP TIME:
15 minutes

 COOKING TIME:
30 minutes

nutritional information per loaf	711 cal, 45g fat, 8.5g sat fat, 31g total sugars, 0.7g salt

Serve with roasted carrots, parsnips, and potatoes for an alternative Christmas feast.

INGREDIENTS

2 tablespoons butter, plus extra for greasing

2 garlic cloves, chopped

1 large onion, chopped

⅓ cup pine nuts, toasted

½ cup hazelnuts, toasted

½ cup walnuts, ground

⅓ cup cashew nuts, ground

2 cups fresh whole-wheat bread crumbs

1 egg, lightly beaten

2 tablespoons chopped fresh thyme, plus extra sprigs to garnish

1 cup vegetable stock

salt and pepper

cranberry & red wine sauce

1¾ cups fresh cranberries

½ cup sugar

1¼ cups red wine

1 cinnamon stick

1. Preheat the oven to 350°F. Grease a loaf pan and line it with wax paper. Melt the butter in a saucepan over medium heat. Add the garlic and onion and cook, stirring, for about 3 minutes. Remove the pan from the heat. Grind the pine nuts and hazelnuts. Stir all the nuts into the pan, add the bread crumbs, egg, thyme, and stock, and season with salt and pepper.

2. Spoon the mixture into the loaf pan and level the surface. Cook in the center of the preheated oven for 30 minutes, or until cooked all the way through and golden. The loaf is cooked when a toothpick inserted into the center comes out clean.

3. Halfway through the cooking time, make the cranberry and red wine sauce. Put all the ingredients in a saucepan and bring to a boil. Reduce the heat and simmer, stirring occasionally, for 15 minutes.

4. Remove the nut roast from the oven and invert. Garnish with sprigs of thyme and serve with the cranberry and red wine sauce.

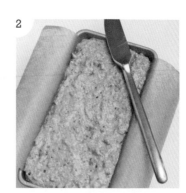

Mushrooms with Garlic & Scallions *98*

Hot & Sour Zucchini *100*

Peas with Lettuce & Tarragon *102*

Roasted Fennel with Tomatoes & Herbs *104*

Spicy Chickpeas *106*

Stir-Fried Broccoli *108*

Spicy Bok Choy with Sesame Sauce *110*

Tomato Rice *112*

Braided Poppy Seed Bread *114*

Tomato & Rosemary Focaccia *116*

Pesto & Olive Soda Bread *118*

Green Leaf & Herb Chutney with Olives *120*

Apricot Smoothie *122*

Celery & Apple Smoothie *124*

Sides

Mushrooms with Garlic & Scallions

 SERVES 4

 PREP TIME:
10 minutes
plus cooling

 COOKING TIME:
1½ hours

nutritional information per serving	80 cal, 6g fat, 1g sat fat, 2g total sugars, trace salt

There may seem to be a huge amount of garlic in this recipe, but don't worry—when you roast whole bulbs in the oven in this way, they become milder, sweeter, and deliciously caramelized.

INGREDIENTS

2 garlic bulbs

2 tablespoons olive oil

12 ounces assorted mushrooms, such as cremini, open-cap, and chanterelles, halved if large

1 tablespoon chopped fresh parsley

8 scallions, cut into 1-inch lengths

salt and pepper

1. Preheat the oven to 350°F. Slice off the tops of the garlic bulbs and press down to loosen the cloves. Place them in an ovenproof dish and season with salt and pepper. Drizzle 2 teaspoons of the oil over the bulbs and roast for 30 minutes. Remove from the oven and drizzle with 1 teaspoon of the remaining oil. Return to the oven and roast for an additional 45 minutes. Remove the garlic from the oven and, when cool enough to handle, peel the cloves.

2. Tip the oil from the dish into a heavy skillet. Add the remaining oil and heat. Add the mushrooms and cook over medium heat, stirring frequently, for 4 minutes.

3. Add the garlic cloves, parsley, and scallions and cook, stirring frequently, for 5 minutes. Season with salt and pepper and serve immediately.

1

1

3

GOES WELL WITH
Serve on toasted
ciabatta bread or
with scrambled
eggs.

Hot & Sour Zucchini

 SERVES 4   PREP TIME: 30 minutes   COOKING TIME: 5 minutes

nutritional information per serving	86 cal, 7g fat, 1.5g sat fat, 4g total sugars, 1.9g salt

In a traditional Sichuan style, this is just one more way to serve the humble zucchini.

INGREDIENTS

2 large zucchini, thinly sliced

1 teaspoon salt

2 tablespoons peanut oil

1 teaspoon Sichuan peppercorns, crushed

½–1 red chile, seeded and sliced into thin strips

1 large garlic clove, thinly sliced

½ teaspoon minced fresh ginger

1 tablespoon rice vinegar

1 tablespoon light soy sauce

2 teaspoons sugar

1 scallion, green part included, thinly sliced

a few drops of sesame oil and 1 teaspoon sesame seeds, to garnish

1. Put the zucchini slices in a large colander and toss with the salt. Cover with a plate and put a weight on top. Let drain for 20 minutes. Rinse off the salt and spread out the slices on paper towels to dry.

2. Preheat a wok over high heat and add the peanut oil. Add the Sichuan peppercorns, chile, garlic, and ginger. Sauté for about 20 seconds, until the garlic is just beginning to color.

3. Add the zucchini slices and toss in the oil. Add the rice vinegar, soy sauce, and sugar, and stir-fry for 2 minutes. Add the scallion and stir-fry for 30 seconds. Garnish with the sesame oil and seeds, and serve immediately.

1

2

3

Peas with Lettuce & Tarragon

 SERVES 4   PREP TIME: 5 minutes    COOKING TIME: 10–15 minutes

nutritional information per serving	162 cal, 8g fat, 3g sat fat, 3g total sugars, trace salt

Transform humble peas into a side dish fit for a dinner party with this quick recipe.

INGREDIENTS

1 tablespoon butter
1 tablespoon olive oil
1 leek, thinly sliced
2 teaspoons all-purpose flour
1 cup vegetable stock
2¼ cups fresh or frozen peas
2 Boston lettuce, sliced
3 tablespoons chopped fresh tarragon
1 tablespoon lemon juice
salt and pepper

1. Heat the butter and oil in a large saucepan. Add the leek, cover, and cook over low heat for 5 minutes, until soft. Stir in the flour, then gradually stir in the stock.

2. Add the peas, increase the heat, cover, and simmer for 4 minutes. Add the lettuce without stirring it in, cover, and simmer for an additional 2 minutes, until the vegetables are tender.

3. Stir the lettuce, tarragon, and lemon juice into the peas. Season with salt and pepper and serve immediately.

SOMETHING
DIFFERENT
To vary the
flavor, replace
the tarragon
with mint or the
lettuce with
frisée endive.

Roasted Fennel with Tomatoes & Herbs

 SERVES 4   PREP TIME: 5 minutes   COOKING TIME: 25–30 minutes

nutritional information per serving	100 cal, 7.5g fat, 1g sat fat, 3g total sugars, 0.2g salt

A wonderful side dish for the summer months when these vegetables are at their cheapest and best.

INGREDIENTS

4 fennel bulbs, cut into slim wedges

2 tablespoons olive oil

⅓ cup dry white wine

2 garlic cloves, crushed

2 teaspoons chopped fresh rosemary

12 cherry tomatoes

16 pitted ripe black olives

2 tablespoons chopped fresh parsley

salt and pepper

1. Preheat the oven to 400°F. Place the fennel in a roasting pan large enough to hold it in a single layer. Mix together the oil, 2 tablespoons of the wine, the garlic, and rosemary. Pour the mixture over the fennel, season with salt and pepper, and toss together.

2. Roast in the preheated oven for 15–20 minutes, until almost tender and lightly browned. Scatter the tomatoes and olives over the fennel. Pour over the remaining wine, then return to the oven for 8–10 minutes, until the tomatoes are soft and the skins have burst. Toss with the parsley and serve warm or cold.

GOES WELL WITH
To turn this side
dish into a light
meal, toss with
couscous and
toasted pine
nuts or with
pasta and
grated vegetarian
Parmesan-style
cheese.

Spicy Chickpeas

 SERVES 4   PREP TIME: 10 minutes   COOKING TIME: 10–12 minutes

nutritional information per serving	190 cal, 2.2g fat, 0.2g sat fat, 10g total sugars, 0.4g salt

This traditional Indian dish goes really well with plain boiled rice and a cucumber raita.

INGREDIENTS

1 (15-ounce) can chickpeas, drained and rinsed
2 Yukon gold or white round potatoes, peeled and diced
2 tablespoons tamarind paste
⅓ cup water
1 teaspoon chili powder
2 teaspoons sugar
1 onion, chopped
salt

to garnish
1 tomato, sliced
2 fresh green chiles, chopped
2–3 tablespoons chopped cilantro

1. Put the drained and rinsed chickpeas in a large bowl.

2. Put the potatoes in a saucepan of water and boil for 10–12 minutes, or until cooked all the way through. Drain and set aside.

3. Mix together the tamarind paste and water in a small bowl.

4. Add the chili powder, sugar, and 1 teaspoon of salt to the tamarind paste mixture and mix together. Pour the mixture over the chickpeas.

5. Add the onion and the diced potatoes, then stir to mix.

6. Transfer to a serving bowl and garnish with tomato, chiles, and chopped cilantro. Serve immediately.

2

5

5

Stir-Fried Broccoli

SERVES 4

PREP TIME:
5 minutes

COOKING TIME:
8–10 minutes

nutritional information
per serving   121 cal, 7.5g fat, 1g sat fat, 6g total sugars, 1.3g salt

Broccoli served this way will tempt everyone to try this great dish, which is equally delicious made with cauliflower or a combination of the two.

INGREDIENTS

2 tablespoons vegetable oil
2 broccoli heads, cut into florets
2 tablespoons soy sauce
1 teaspoon cornstarch
1 tablespoon sugar
1 teaspoon grated fresh ginger
1 garlic clove, crushed
pinch of crushed red pepper
1 teaspoon toasted sesame seeds,
to garnish

1. Heat the oil in a large, preheated wok or skillet over high heat until almost smoking. Add the broccoli and stir-fry for 4–5 minutes. Reduce the heat to medium.

2. Combine the soy sauce, cornstarch, sugar, ginger, garlic, and crushed red pepper in a small bowl. Add the mixture to the broccoli and cook, stirring continuously, for 2–3 minutes, until the sauce thickens slightly.

3. Transfer to a warm serving dish, garnish with the sesame seeds, and serve immediately.

1

2

2

HEALTHY HINT
If you prefer,
you could steam
the broccoli for
3-4 minutes,
until tender.

Spicy Bok Choy
with Sesame Sauce

 SERVES 4   PREP TIME: 10 minutes   COOKING TIME: 8–10 minutes

nutritional information per serving	163 cal, 14g fat, 2g sat fat, 4.5g total sugars, 1.7g salt

There are various spellings of bok choy, a member of the cabbage family. Choose the smaller, more tender ones with perky leaves and unblemished stems.

INGREDIENTS

2 teaspoons peanut oil or vegetable oil

1 red chile, seeded and thinly sliced

1 garlic clove, thinly sliced

5 small bok choys, quartered

½ cup vegetable stock

sauce

2½ tablespoons sesame seeds

2 tablespoons dark soy sauce

2 teaspoons light brown sugar

1 garlic clove, crushed

3 tablespoons sesame oil

1. For the sesame sauce, toast the sesame seeds in a dry skillet set over medium heat, stirring until lightly browned. Remove from the heat and cool slightly. Transfer to a mortar and pestle. Add the soy sauce, sugar, and crushed garlic and pound to a coarse paste. Stir in the sesame oil.

2. Heat the peanut oil in a wok or large skillet. Add the chile and sliced garlic and stir-fry for 20–30 seconds. Add the bok choy and stir-fry for 5 minutes, adding the stock a little at a time to prevent sticking.

3. Transfer the bok choy to a warm dish, drizzle the sesame sauce over the top, and serve immediately.

1

2

2

Tomato Rice

 SERVES 4   PREP TIME: 10 minutes   COOKING TIME: 25–30 minutes

nutritional information per serving	210 cal, 1g fat, 0.1g sat fat, 4g total sugars, trace salt

Colorful tomato-flavored rice is great for serving to the family with a wide selection of main dishes.

INGREDIENTS

1 onion, chopped

6 plum tomatoes, peeled, seeded, and chopped

1 cup vegetable stock

1 cup long-grain rice

salt and pepper

1. Put the onion and tomatoes in a food processor and process to a smooth puree. Scrape the puree into a saucepan, pour in the stock, and bring to a boil over medium heat, stirring occasionally.

2. Add the rice and stir once, then reduce the heat, cover, and simmer for 20–25 minutes, until all the liquid has been absorbed and the rice is tender. Season with salt and pepper and serve immediately.

SOMETHING
DIFFERENT
Serve with your
favorite chili
sauce if you
like some heat.

Braided Poppy Seed Bread

 MAKES
1 loaf

 PREP TIME:
20 minutes
plus rising

 COOKING TIME:
30–35 minutes

nutritional information per loaf	1,342 cal, 85g fat, 14g sat fat, 56g total sugars, 4.6g salt

For a change of pace, use other seeds, such as sesame, onion, or pumpkin, instead of poppy.

INGREDIENTS

1¾ cups white bread flour, plus extra for dusting

1 teaspoon salt

2 tablespoons instant skim milk powder

1½ tablespoons sugar

1 teaspoon active dry yeast

¾ cup lukewarm water

2 tablespoons vegetable oil, plus extra for greasing

⅓ cup poppy seeds

topping
1 egg yolk

1 tablespoon milk

1 tablespoon sugar

2 tablespoons poppy seeds

1. Sift the flour and salt together into a bowl and stir in the milk powder, sugar, and yeast. Make a well in the center, pour in the water and oil, and stir until the dough begins to come together. Add the poppy seeds and knead until completely combined and the dough leaves the side of the bowl. Invert onto a lightly floured surface and knead well for about 10 minutes, until smooth and elastic.

2. Brush a bowl with oil. Shape the dough into a ball, put it in the bowl, and place the bowl in a plastic bag or cover with a damp dish towel. Let rise in a warm place for 1 hour, or until doubled in volume.

3. Oil a baking sheet. Invert the dough onto a lightly floured surface and knead for 1–2 minutes. Divide into three equal pieces and shape each into a rope 10–12 inches long. Place the ropes side by side and press together at one end. Braid the dough, pinch the other end together, and tuck underneath.

4. Put the loaf on the prepared baking sheet, cover, and let rise in a warm place for 30 minutes. Meanwhile, preheat the oven to 400°F.

5. For the topping, beat the egg yolk with the milk and sugar. Brush the egg glaze over the top of the loaf and sprinkle with the poppy seeds. Bake in the preheated oven for 30–35 minutes, until golden brown. Transfer to a wire rack and Let cool.

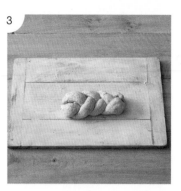

3

5

Tomato & Rosemary Focaccia

 MAKES 1 loaf

 PREP TIME: 20 minutes plus rising

 COOKING TIME: 25–30 minutes

nutritional information per loaf	1,742 cal, 60g fat, 9g sat fat, 16g total sugars, 11g salt

A simplified version of the classic loaf studded with roasted cherry tomatoes and aromatic rosemary.

INGREDIENTS

⅓ cup olive oil, plus extra for greasing

2 garlic cloves, crushed

2½ cups white bread flour, plus extra for kneading

2¼ teaspoons active dry yeast

2 teaspoons table salt

1 teaspoon sugar

1 cup lukewarm water

2 teaspoons finely chopped fresh rosemary

12–14 ripe red cherry tomatoes

¼ teaspoon flaky sea salt

1. Mix 2 tablespoons of the oil with all of the garlic. Set aside. Mix together the flour, yeast, table salt, and sugar in a large bowl. Add the remaining oil and water. Mix to a dough. Invert onto a lightly floured surface and knead for 10 minutes, until smooth and elastic, then knead in 1 tablespoon of the garlic-flavored oil.

2. Oil a rectangular baking pan measuring about 6½ x 10 inches and at least 1½ inches deep. Press the dough over the bottom of the pan with your hands. Brush with the remaining garlic oil, then sprinkle with the rosemary. Cover loosely with plastic wrap and set aside in a warm place for about 1 hour, until puffed up and doubled in size.

3. Preheat the oven to 450°F. Place the tomatoes on the focaccia (squeeze in as many as you can) and press them into the dough. Sprinkle with the sea salt. Place in the preheated oven and immediately reduce the temperature to 400°F. Bake for 25–30 minutes, until golden brown and the center sounds hollow when tapped. Invert onto a wire rack to cool. Serve warm or cold.

1

2

3

COOK'S NOTE
If you don't have a deep baking pan, press out the dough to about the same size on an oiled baking sheet.

Pesto & Olive Soda Bread

 MAKES
1 loaf

 PREP TIME:
15 minutes

 COOKING TIME:
30–35 minutes

nutritional information per loaf	2,156 cal, 43g fat, 4g sat fat, 21g total sugars, 6.7g salt

If you're not confident about baking with yeast, try this recipe—you're guaranteed to have great results. Use one of the pestos available in the supermarket or make your own. Either way, you will have a loaf to be proud of.

INGREDIENTS

olive oil, for greasing
2 cups all-purpose flour
2 cups whole-wheat flour
1 teaspoon baking soda
½ teaspoon salt
3 tablespoons pesto
about 1¼ cups buttermilk
½ cup coarsely chopped, pitted green olives,
milk, for glazing

1. Preheat the oven to 400°F and line and grease a baking sheet. Sift the flours, baking soda, and salt into a bowl, adding back any bran from the sifter.

2. Mix the pesto and buttermilk. Stir into the flour with the olives, mixing to a soft dough. Add more liquid, if needed.

3. Shape the dough into an 8-inch circle and place on the baking sheet. Flatten slightly and cut a deep cross with a sharp knife.

4. Brush with milk and bake in the preheated oven for 30–35 minutes, until golden brown. The loaf should sound hollow when tapped underneath. Transfer to a wire rack to cool.

1

2

3

Green Leaf & Herb Chutney with Olives

 SERVES 4 PREP TIME: 10 minutes plus cooling  COOKING TIME: 15–20 minutes

nutritional information per serving	95 cal, 9.5g fat, 1.5g sat fat, 1g total sugars, 0.3g salt

With a vibrant green color and zingy combination of herbs and spices, this is perfect spread on bread, but it is equally good as a dip or accompaniment to main meals.

INGREDIENTS

1 (8-ounce) package fresh baby spinach

handful of celery leaves

3 tablespoons olive oil

2–3 garlic cloves, crushed

1 teaspoon cumin seeds

6–8 ripe black olives, pitted and finely chopped

1 large bunch of fresh flat-leaf parsley leaves, finely chopped

1 large bunch of cilantro leaves, finely chopped

1 teaspoon smoked paprika

juice of ½ lemon

salt and pepper

toasted flatbread or crusty bread and ripe black olives, to serve

1. Put the spinach and celery leaves in a steamer and steam until tender. Refresh the leaves under cold running water, drain well, and squeeze out the excess water. Place the steamed leaves on a wooden cutting board and chop to a pulp.

2. Heat 2 tablespoons of the oil in a heavy casserole dish. Add the garlic and cumin seeds, then cook over medium heat for 1–2 minutes, stirring, until they emit a nutty aroma. Stir in the olives with the parsley and cilantro, then add the paprika.

3. Toss in the pulped spinach and celery and cook over low heat, stirring occasionally, for 10 minutes, until the mixture is smooth and compact. Season with salt and pepper and let cool.

4. Transfer the mixture to a bowl and bind with the remaining oil and the lemon juice. Serve with toasted flatbread or crusty bread and olives.

Apricot Smoothie

 SERVES 2   PREP TIME: 5 minutes   COOKING TIME: No cooking

nutritional information per serving	52 cal, 0.2g fat, 0g sat fat, 11g total sugars, trace salt

When apricots are ripe and bursting with flavor, this Asian inspired "mocktail" will really go down well. Serve with ice on a warm summer morning.

INGREDIENTS

6 apricots
1 orange
1 fresh lemongrass stalk
¾-inch piece fresh ginger, peeled
ice cubes, to serve

1. Halve and pit the apricots. Peel the orange, leaving some of the white pith. Cut the lemongrass into chunks.

2. Put the apricots, orange, lemongrass, and ginger in a food processor or juicer and blend together all the ingredients. Pour the mixture into glasses, add ice, and serve.

1

2

2

Celery & Apple Smoothie

nutritional information per serving	225 cal, 12g fat, 7g sat fat, 20g total sugars, 0.5g salt

A milkshake that does you good! Celery and apple are the perfect combination in this drink, which is great on hot summer days. Serve in tall glasses with strips of celery to decorate.

INGREDIENTS

3 celery stalks, chopped

1 apple, such as Golden Delicious, Empire, or Fuji, peeled, cored, and diced

2½ cups milk

pinch of sugar (optional)

salt (optional)

strips of celery, for decorating

1. Put the celery, apple, and milk in a blender and process until thoroughly combined.

2. Stir in the sugar and some salt, if using. Pour into chilled glasses, decorate with strips of celery, and serve.

1

2

2

Index